Community, Culture, and Me

Written by
Gavin Worthy

Types of Communities

KidHaven
PUBLISHING

Published in 2027 by
KidHaven Publishing, an Imprint of Greenhaven Publishing, LLC
2544 Clinton St., Buffalo, NY 14224

Written by: Gavin Worthy
Edited by: Doug Barone
Designed by: Ker Ker Lee

All facts, statistics, web addresses, and URLs in this book were verified as valid and accurate at time of writing. No responsibility for any changes to external websites or references can be accepted by either the author or publisher.

Cataloging-in-Publication Data

Names: Worthy, Gavin.
Title: Types of communities / Gavin Worthy.
Description: Buffalo, NY : KidHaven Publishing, 2027. | Series: Community, culture, and me | Includes glossary and index.
Identifiers: ISBN 9781534569959 (pbk.) | ISBN 9781534569966 (library bound) | ISBN 9781534569973 (ebook)
Subjects: LCSH: Communities--Juvenile literature. | Community organization--Juvenile literature.
Classification: LCC HM756.W678 2027 | DDC 307--dc23

Printed in China

CPSIA compliance information: Batch #QS27KH: For further information contact Greenhaven Publishing LLC at 1-844-317-7404.

Photo Credits – Images courtesy of Shutterstock.com, unless otherwise stated.

Cover & Recurring – Rawpixel.com, PeopleImages.com, Dedraw Studio, TVhappyLine. 2–3 – PeopleImages. 4–5 – Kitreel, Rawpixel.com. 6–7 – ymgerman, Monkey Business Images. 8–9 – Jellygoround, DC Studio. 10–11 – ClaudiaRamirezValdespino, Dean Drobot, Riccardo Mayer. 12–13 – SHEE HENG CHONG, BearFotos. 14–15 – Gagarin Iurii, NataliaCatalina.com. 16–17 – Atif Amin, Wirestock Creators. 18–19 – jianbing Lee, SpeedKingz. 20–21 – ideadesign, New Africa. 22–23 – Prapon Srinakara, matimix.

Contents

Words that look like **this** can be found in the glossary on page 24.

All Together Now

A community is a group of people who have something in common. A community could be made up of people from the same village or people who enjoy the same hobby.

Can you think of a community you belong to?

Being part of a community means sharing and helping each other. Think of a project at school—it is much easier when everyone helps. In a community, everybody helps in their own way.

Communities in the City

A city is one big community. It is also made up of many smaller **neighborhood** communities too. People might live very close together in a city community.

a city in Australia

Some buildings are important parts of city communities. Libraries, parks, schools, and community centers are places where people can meet. The community can share these places and come together.

Countryside Communities

There may be smaller communities in the countryside. A community might be made up of people from a village. Village halls, marketplaces, or open spaces can be important places for the community.

The people in a village community often rely on each other. Neighbors might all know and help each other. This makes the community an important part of everyone's lives.

A Community for Who You Are

Your identity is all the things that make you who you are. This might include your age, what you wear, your beliefs, and your race. What makes up your identity?

Communities can be made up of people who share part of their identity. People can feel connected to others who are like them in some way, even if they are not from the same town or city.

Religion

If someone follows a religion, it means they believe in a spiritual power. This usually means believing in a god or many gods. Communities can include people who follow the same religion.

There can be many smaller communities within larger religious communities.

Many religions have important buildings, called places of worship. These are places where members of the community can see each other. People can worship and celebrate together.

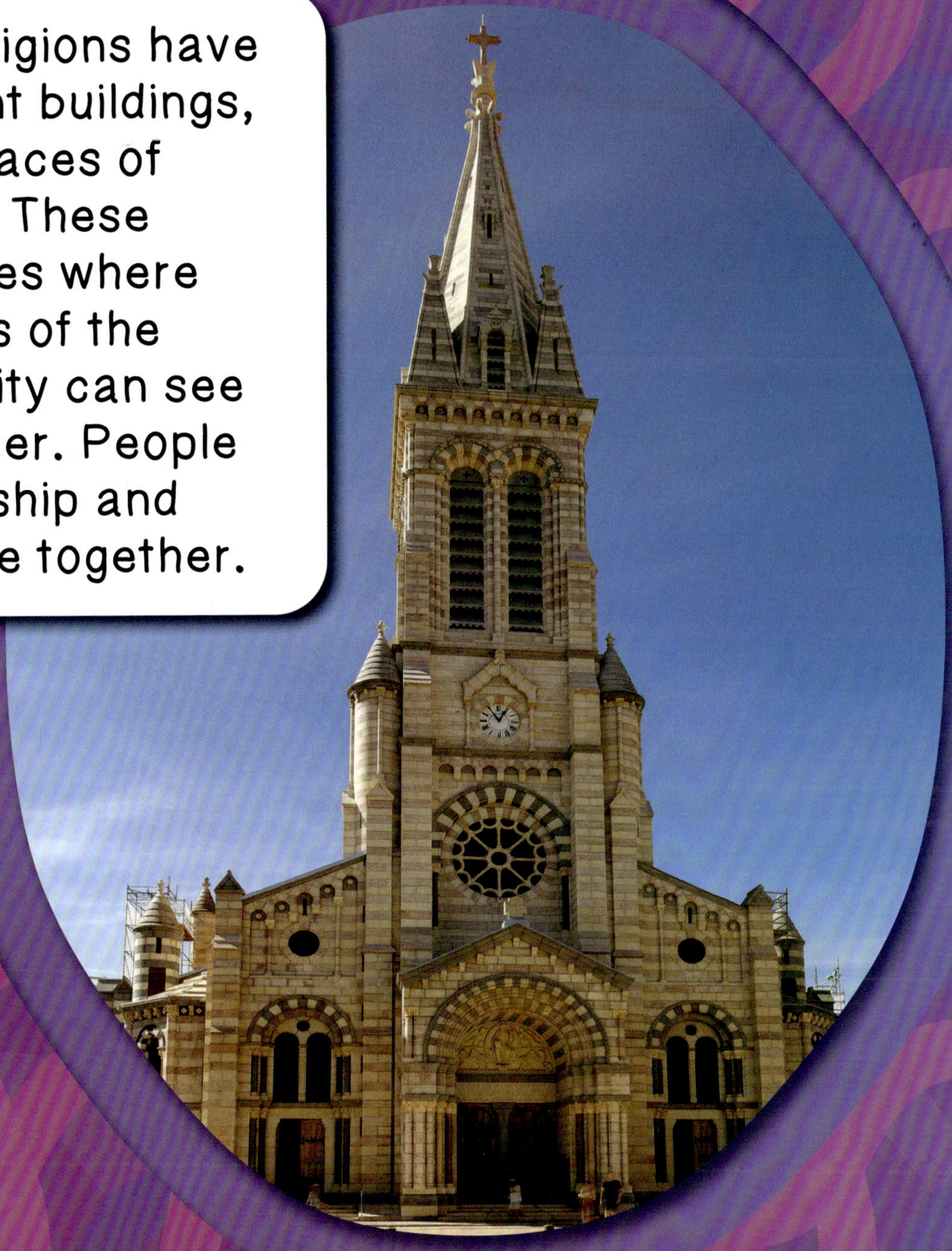

Art Communities

Art can mean lots of things. Music, painting, dancing, writing stories, and sculpting are all types of art. People who make art build communities too. They help each other by sharing ideas or giving money.

Members of an art community can work on a project together.

You do not have to be a rich and famous artist to belong to an art community. Anyone can be part of an art community if they like creating art.

A **local** music scene can be an art community.

Sports

A community can be built around people who enjoy sports. This might be a group of people who support a certain team. It could also be a group of people who play sports together.

Sports fields are an important place for sports communities. People can meet and **bond** with each other, as well as watch and play sports.

These cricket grounds in India are an important place for the cricket community.

School Communities

Whatever kind of school you go to, you belong to your school community. A school can be made up of lots of smaller communities too. For example, your class is a community.

School clubs can be important places to bond with others. In some schools around the world, children clean the school together. It is important to look after the people and places in your community.

School drama club

The Planet Is a Community

The global community includes everyone on Earth. This is the biggest type of community there is. Everyone shares the same planet, and we also share the **responsibility** of taking care of it.

There are lots of ways to protect the planet.

Climate change is a problem for everyone, and the global community must work together to solve it. By caring for Earth, we are caring for every person, animal, and plant that lives here.

It Starts With You

You can be part of lots of different communities at once—you don't have to choose one. Can you think of some communities that you are already part of?

If you would like to join new communities or get more involved with others, there are lots of places to start. Check out events at your school or your local library.

Maybe you would like to build a new community—it starts with you!

Glossary

bond	to form a relationship based on love, friendship, or loyalty
climate change	a change in the typical weather or temperature of a large area over a long time
identity	a person's views of who they are
local	describing the area near where someone lives
neighborhood	an area within a town or city where people live near each other
responsibility	the need to do certain things which are usually good or helpful
sculpting	making an object or statue out of a material such as clay
spiritual	related to something that is beyond a world that can be sensed, and can be related to religion
worship	religious acts of praise, such as prayer

Index